DRAWING THE SIX DIRECTIONS

PREVIOUSLY BY EILEEN R. TABIOS

POETRY

After The Egyptians Determined The Shape of the World Is A Circle, 1996
Beyond Life Sentences, 1998
The Empty Flagpole (CD with guest artist Mei-mei Berssenbrugge), 2000
Ecstatic Mutations (with short stories and essays), 2001
Reproductions of The Empty Flagpole, 2002
Enheduanna in the 21st Century, 2002
There, Where the Pages Would End, 2003
Menage a Trois With the 21st Century, 2004
Crucial Bliss Epilogues, 2004
The Estrus Gaze(s), 2005
Songs of the Colon, 2005
Post Bling Bling, 2005
I Take Thee, English, For My Beloved, 2005
The Secret Lives of Punctuations, Vol. I, 2006
Dredging for Atlantis, 2006
It's Curtains, 2006
SILENCES: The Autobiography of Loss, 2007
The Singer and Others: Flamenco Hay(na)ku, 2007
The Light Sang As It Left Your Eyes: Our Autobiography, 2007
Nota Bene Eiswein, 2009
Footnotes to Algebra: Uncollected Poems 1995-2009, 2009
On A Pyre: An Ars Poetica, 2010
Roman Holiday, 2010
Hay(na)ku for Haiti, 2010
THE THORN ROSARY: Selected Prose Poems and New 1998-2010, 2010
the relational elations of ORPHANED ALGEBRA (with j/j hastain), 2012
5 Shades of Gray, 2012
THE AWAKENING: A Long Poem Triptych & A Poetics Fragment, 2013
147 Million Orphans (MMXI-MML), 2014
44 RESURRECTIONS, 2014
SUN STIGMATA (Sculpture Poems), 2014
I Forgot Light Burns, 2015
Duende in the Alleys, 2015
INVENT(ST)ORY: Selected Catalog Poems & New (1996-2015), 2015
The Connoisseur of Alleys, 2016
The Gilded Age of Kickstarters, 2016
Excavating the Filipino in Me, 2016
I Forgot Ars Poetica, 2016
AMNESIA: Somebody's Memoir, 2016
THE OPPOSITE OF CLAUSTROPHOBIA: Prime's Anti-Autobiography, 2017
Post-Ecstasy Mutations, 2017
On Green Lawn, The Scent of White, 2017
To Be An Empire Is To Burn, 2017
If They Hadn't Worn White Hoods … (with John Bloomberg-Rissman), 2017
What Shivering Monks Comprehend, 2017
YOUR FATHER IS BALD: Selected Hay(na)ku Poems, 2017

IMMIGRANT: Hay(na)ku & Other Poems In A New Land, 2017
Comprehending Mortality (with John Bloomberg-Rissman), 2017
Big City Cante Intermedio, 2017
WINTER ON WALL STREET: A Novella-in-Verse, 2017
Making National Poetry Month Great Again, 2017
MANHATTAN: An Archaeology, 2017
Love In A Time of Belligerence, 2017
MURDER DEATH RESURRECTION: A Poetry Generator, 2018
TANKA, Vol. I, 2018
HIRAETH: Tercets From The Last Archipelago, 2018
One, Two, Three: Selected Hay(na)ku Poems (Trans. Rebeka Lembo), 2018
THE GREAT AMERICAN NOVEL: Selected Visual Poetry 2001-2019, 2019
The In(ter)vention of the Hay(na)ku: Selected Tercets 1996-2019, 2019 & 2021
Witness in the Convex Mirror, 2019
Evocare: Selected Tankas (with Ayo Gutierrez and Brian Cain Anne), 2019
We Are It, 2020
Inculpatory Evidence: The Covid-19 Poems, 2020
Political Love, 2021
La Vie érotique de l'art, une séance avec William Carlos Williams (Trad. de l'anglais (États-Unis) par Samuel Rochery), 2021
PRISES (Trad. de l'anglais (États-Unis) par Fanny Garin), 2022
Because I Love You, I Become War, 2023
Drawing the Six Directions, 2024

FICTION

Behind The Blue Canvas, 2004
Novel Chatelaine, 2009
SILK EGG: Collected Novels 2009-2009, 2011
What Counts, 2020
PAGPAG: The Dictator's Aftermath in the Diaspora, 2020
DOVELION: A Fairy Tale for Our Times, 2021
Simmering: a novella-in-prose-poems, 2022
Getting to One, flash fictions with art by harry k stammer, 2023

PROSE COLLECTIONS

Black Lightning: Poetry-In-Progress (poetry essays/interviews), 1998
My Romance (art essays with poems), 2002
The Blind Chatelaine's Keys (biography with haybun), 2008
AGAINST MISANTHROPY: A Life in Poetry (2015-1995), 2015
#EileenWritesNovel, 2017
Tiny Stickers: A Covid-19 Autobiography, 2020
THE INVENTOR: A Poet's Transcolonial Autobiography, 2023

DRAWING THE SIX DIRECTIONS

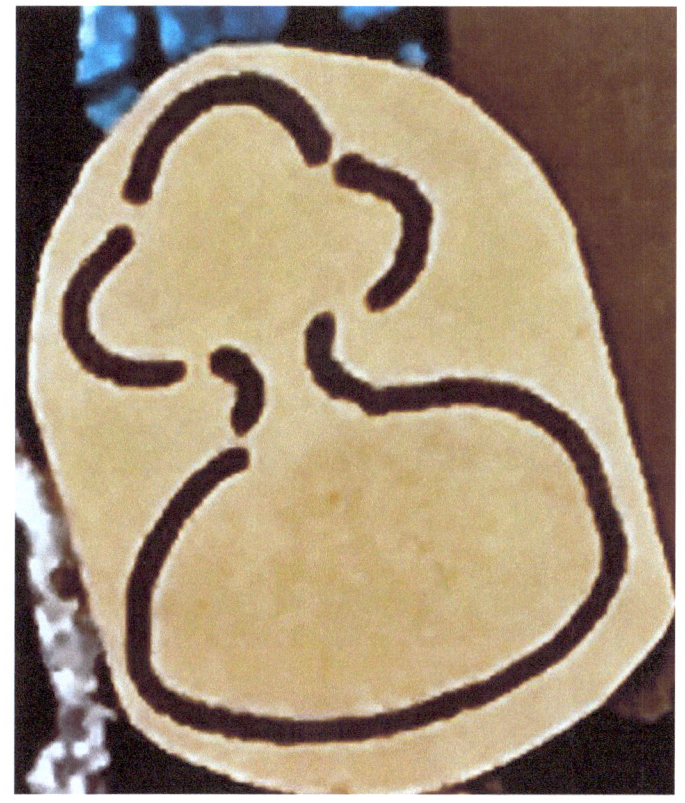

Eileen R. Tabios

Sandy Press

Copyright © 2024 by Eileen Tabios

All rights reserved. No part of this book may be reproduced or transmitted in any form or by any means graphic, electronic or mechanical, including photocopying, recording, taping or by any information storage or retrieval system, without the permission in writing from the Copyright holders.

Cover design, cover preparation, & interior layout by harry k stammer

ISBN: 978-1-7368160-9-7

Printed in U.S.A.

Sandy Press

Acknowledgments

My deep gratitude to those who helped make this book possible: harry k stammer and Mark Young of Sandy Press; Joey Ayala, Michelle Bautista, Barbara Jane Reyes, and Malou Babilonia for making possible the exhibition of "Six Directions" at Pusod Gallery (Berkeley, CA); Marsh Hawk Press for first publishing about the "Six Directions" project in my book *I Take Thee, English, for My Beloved* (2005); and Editors Kristine Snodgrass and Karla Van Vliet for including three drawings in *Glitchy Woman: An anthology of women glitching in 2022-23 (Dusie Press 2024)*.

Articles about the "Six Directions" project were published in *Creative Insight: Fine Arts and Poetry, Factorial, Interlope and the San Francisco Bay Guardian*.

CONTENTS

Introduction 9

Drawings Form/From The Six Directions 17

The Glitchy Mini-Folio 37

Selected Poems From The Six Direction*s* 45

Afterword: Poems From The Six Directions 69

About the Poet 83

Introduction

DRAWINGS FORM/FROM THE SIX DIRECTIONS

I consider *Poetry* to be a practice, a way of living. For me, living as a poet requires maximizing awareness of the world in order to be effective as a poet. By "effective," I refer to my hope that my poems create spaces for experiences that its readers find meaningful, if not pleasurable. In attempting to reach as many readers as possible, I consider attentiveness important for noticing, understanding, and analyzing elements that then may be incorporated into poems. I believe that the more that a poet educates one's self—the more that a poet *sees!*—the more likely that a poet will be able to respect and reach many among the different peoples who exist in our universe of diverse cultures, personalities, styles, and contexts.

Consequently, working to expand the cultural presence of poetry has been an integral part of my activities as a poet. I not only write but also work as an editor, cultural activist, publisher, mentor, and critic—all to promote poetry. My attempts to *live* instead of just *write* poetry resulted in a multidisciplinary and interactive project entitled "Poems Form/From the Six Directions." This 2002 project encompassed several performances, exhibitions, and readings in California's Bay Area (San Francisco, Berkeley, and Sonoma). Because I'd focused then on the interactive aspects of the project—befitting my concern to involve, thus expand, the audience for poetry—the project's least known element is a series of drawings (featured in this book), most of which have never been seen in public.

Six Directions is a Native American concept of the directions consisting of north, south, east, west, up and down—it was introduced to me by poet and New Mexico resident Arthur Sze. The concept resonates in terms of how its multidimensionality reflects my belief that poems are not just words lying flat on the page but are living—*breath*-ing!—creatures. My Six Directions project began in part when I was trying to envision the visual equivalent of a poem. I had been considering the saying, "Poetry is not words but what lies between words, between the lines." Because the statement implies that poetry is invisible, I wondered what a poem's "body" might look like and determined to answer my own question by "sculpting" poems. I thought of the sculptural process because sculptures are three-dimensional (versus lying flatly against the one-dimensional field of a page). Thus, I created mixed-media sculptures whose processes also engendered verse-poems. Through the Six Directions approach, I ended up with poems that work as texts on the page as well as objects that symbolize the three+-dimensional bodies of poems.

Multidimensionality is relevant to my position as a Filipino in the diaspora. I am someone forced to find "Home" beyond the border of the Philippines as well as someone for whom "Philippines" has become a state of mind rather than the actual country that exists today, given its many upheavals that have taken place since my childhood there in the 1960s. So, in defining "Home," I wanted to integrate ALL (or as much) of the world into myself. For instance, I related to a Native American concept (rather than an indigenous Filipino concept) to title this series. The title is appropriate because, as a diasporic Filipino, I wish to be open to all cultures. Well, and I believe a poet should be open, in any event, to all possibilities of human life.

But Six Directions also began because I was trying to create a poem in a new way. For years, I had written "abstract" poetry as a way to avoid narrative poems. This relates to how English was used as a colonizing tool in the Philippines; it is a history that made me reluctant to rely on narrative in my poems because, for me, narrative evokes how English as a communications tool served the expansion of U.S.-American imperialism in the Philippines.

Thus, I wanted to try something different than abstract poetry, and yet didn't wish to fall back to narrative. Creating mixed-media sculptures whose processes engendered verse-poems fit that impetus.

Unexpectedly, however, the sculpting process made me focus for the first time on working with physical material. As a writer working with imagination and words, I was surprised by the pleasurable frisson of dealing with the tangible: the found materials that made their way into my mixed-media sculptures (e.g. old coasters, used magazines, ribbons, recycled cardboard and so on). The sculpting process created a simmer in my belly, like the physical effect that I often feel when I am chasing down a poem into written form. I, therefore, decided to try my own hand at working more consciously as a visual artist. I hadn't planned to go this route when I began Six Directions, but allowed myself to follow the impulse as I realized that this opening manifested what is wonderful about all Art and Poetry: how they can lead its maker and viewer/reader into new experiences.

I created about a dozen sculptures before sculpting led me to drawing. Because I was new as well at this media, I didn't have any drawing-related materials like sketching pads. I began by drawing on what was available to me: brown paper bags that were piling up in my kitchen. As an environmentalist, I was pleased with being able to reuse the bags! But I also appreciated the paper bags because they were found objects. As with the found material that comprised my earlier sculptures, the inclusion of found objects symbolize how I integrate (elements of) the world into my work. The paper bags came to form an installation, "The Brown Paper Bag Series," consisting of 19 paper bag drawings and which later was exhibited at the Pusod gallery in Berkeley, CA.

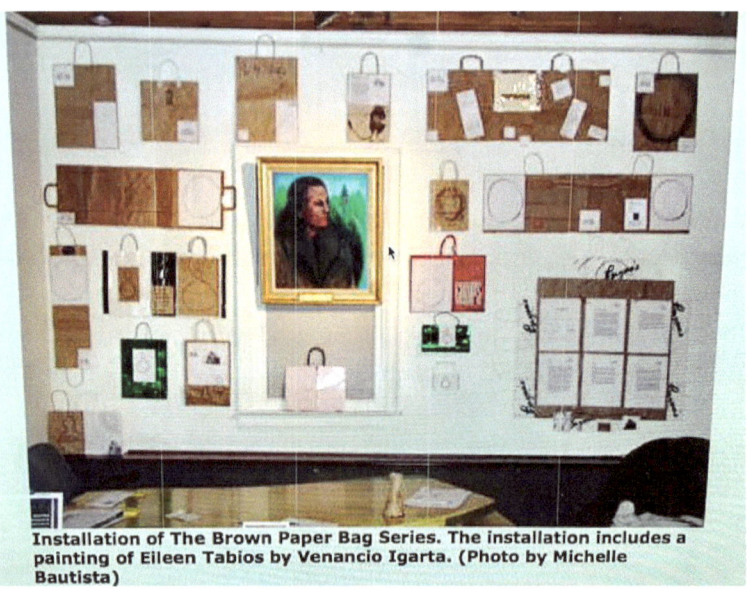

Installation of The Brown Paper Bag Series. The installation includes a painting of Eileen Tabios by Venancio Igarta. (Photo by Michelle Bautista)

The brown color of the paper bags also evoke the notion of Filipino *kayumangi* (brown) skin; as such, they encouraged me to visually explore my identity as a Filipino poet. For the early drawings, I drew many circles because the circle is a simple image, something that my untrained hands could at least attempt. However, I was uneasy with the circle because I related it more to the *enso*, the Japanese word for circle (at the time, I was spending much time with Max Gimblett, a Buddhist artist who frequently painted/drew the *enso*). I didn't yet know what the *enso* had to do with me (except for providing an archetypal image that I love). Fortunately, with more time, I came to transform the circle into an abstracted outline of a vegetable gourd— this abstracted icon is a humanized small circle atop a larger circle.

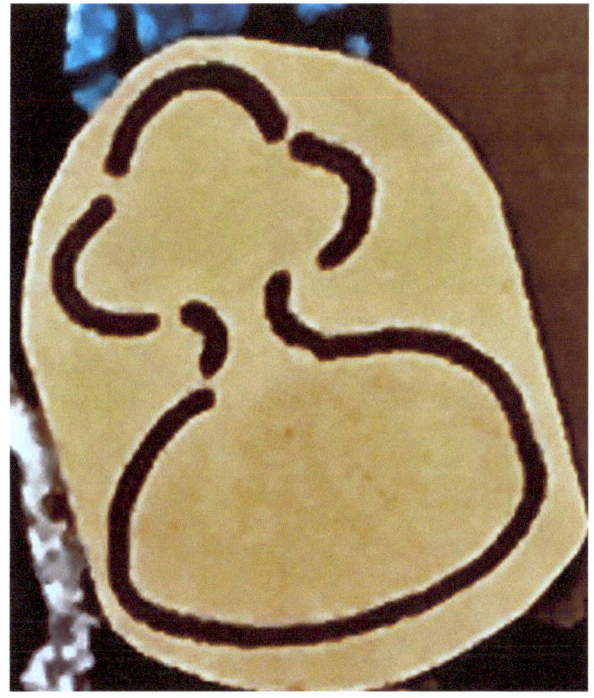

The gourd image references certain indigenous myths that describe how the first or certain humans came out of a cracked gourd(s). Thus, for me, the gourd image came to symbolize "Filipino poet." It is worth noting, however, that my gourd icon did not erase but only incorporated the reference to the *enso*. This is significant because I believe the exploration of one's identity or culture is not synonymous with rejecting other cultures. As well, because the Philippines' history is a diasporic one, it seems logical that non-Filipino elements can integrate themselves into the process of exploring Filipino identity.

In my Six Directions drawings, my drawing "mark" is consistently the gourd icon. For example, if I drew a horizon, I would use tiny gourd images lined up closely together to form a horizontal line. I created nearly 30 such drawings (including the drawings in this publication).

Tellingly, as I created this series of drawings, I began to appreciate drawing based on its own nature, not as a means to something else (such as writing a poem). Drawing just to draw. That's when I began to make larger works on drawing paper which was larger than the typical shopping bags I was then using. As well, I became interested in drawing space, as demarcated by the contrasting visibility of my gourd-based marks. I also made colored drawings as stand-alone works so that I could focus on color which I began introducing into my works.

With hindsight, this all seems fitting: by coming to relate to drawing based on drawing's own nature, I took on a more respectful approach to the media. I ended up paying more direct attention to the nature of drawing itself—to seeing drawing for itself rather than as a tool for another interest. If you wish to respect someone or something, it's best to see them for what they are rather than through your own biases or preconceptions. This whole process made me respect—then more appreciate—drawing as its own form. It's an appropriate result: whether it's for other cultures or for the nature of physical material, *respect* is an integral concept underlying "Poems Form/From The Six Directions."

Visual art enhances the ways to see. Drawings taught me: the wider the expanse of lucidity, the more likely respect will arise. The way is multi-dimensional. The way is worthwhile.

Respectfully,

Eileen R. Tabios

DRAWINGS FORM/FROM THE SIX DIRECTIONS

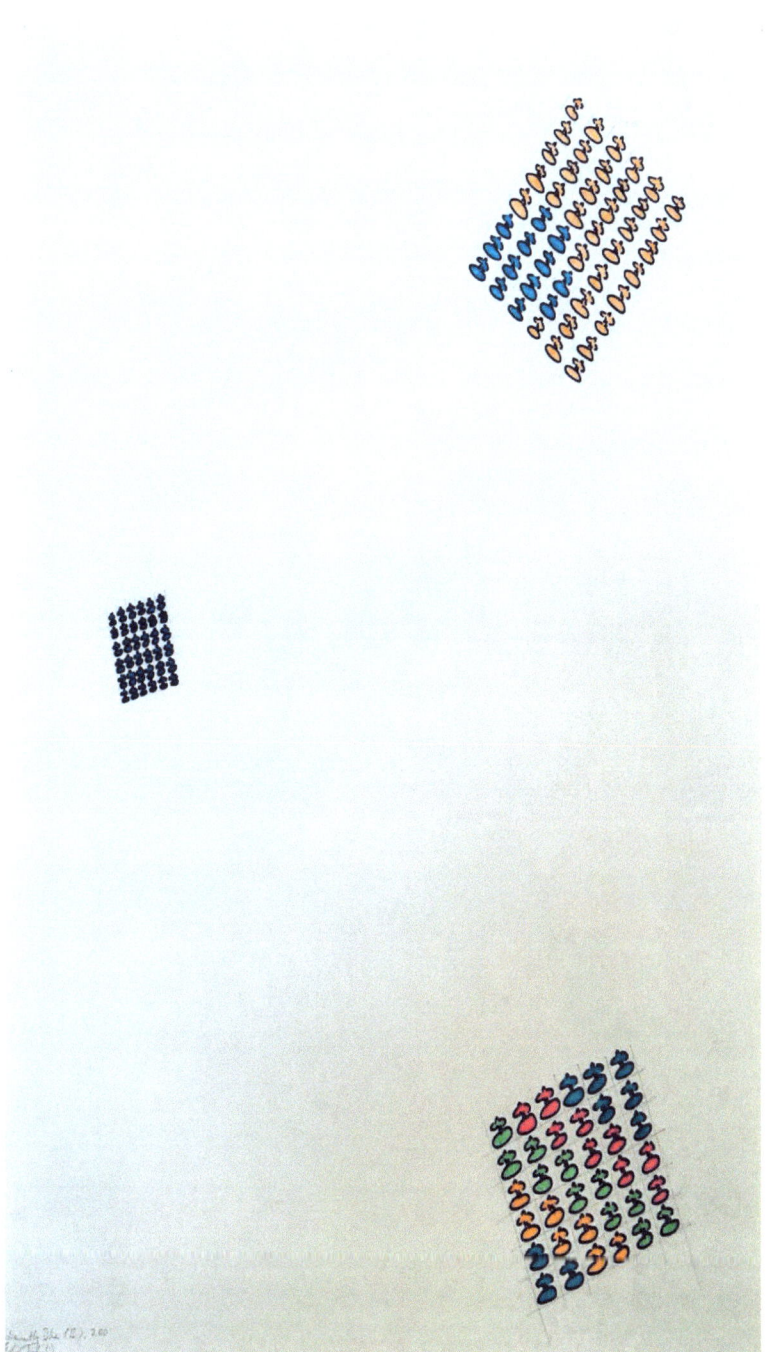

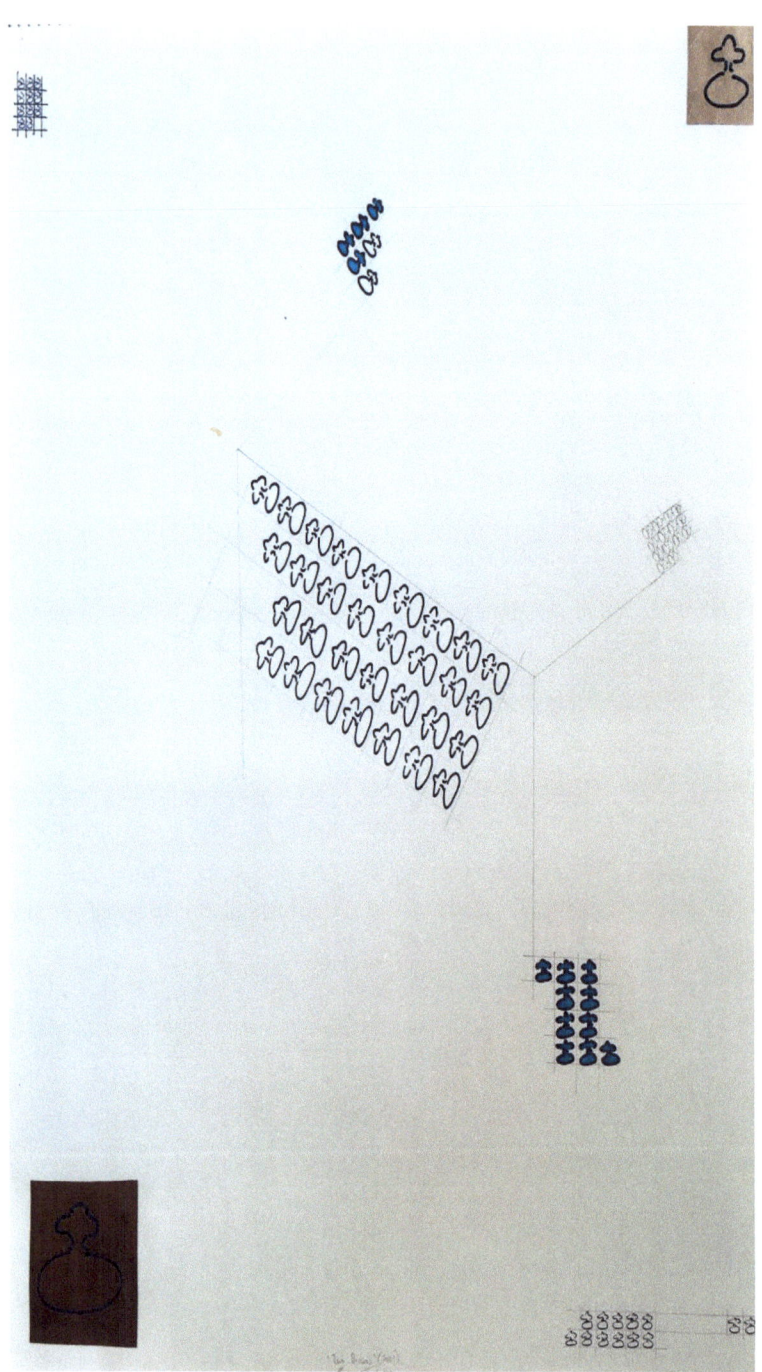

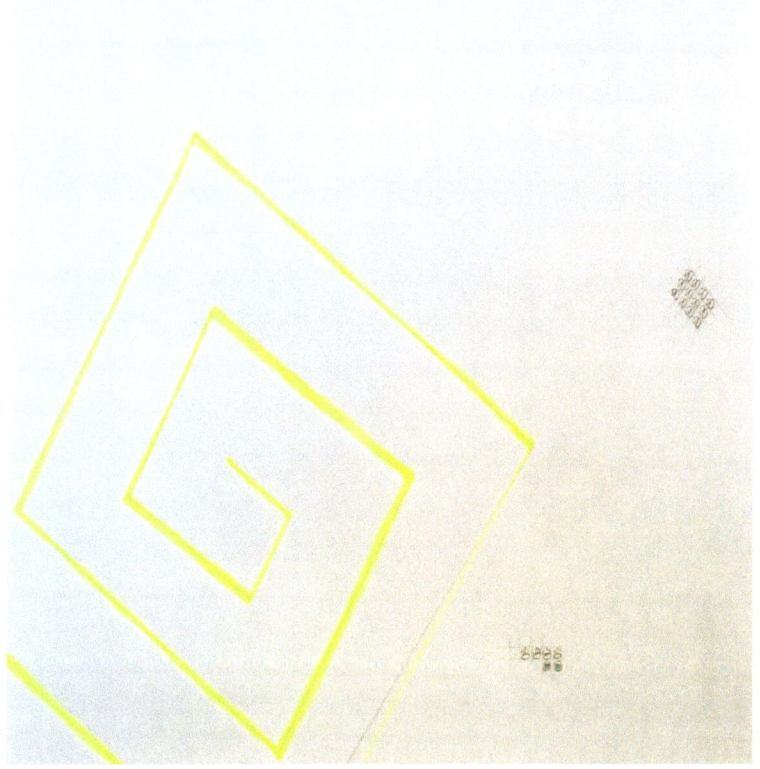

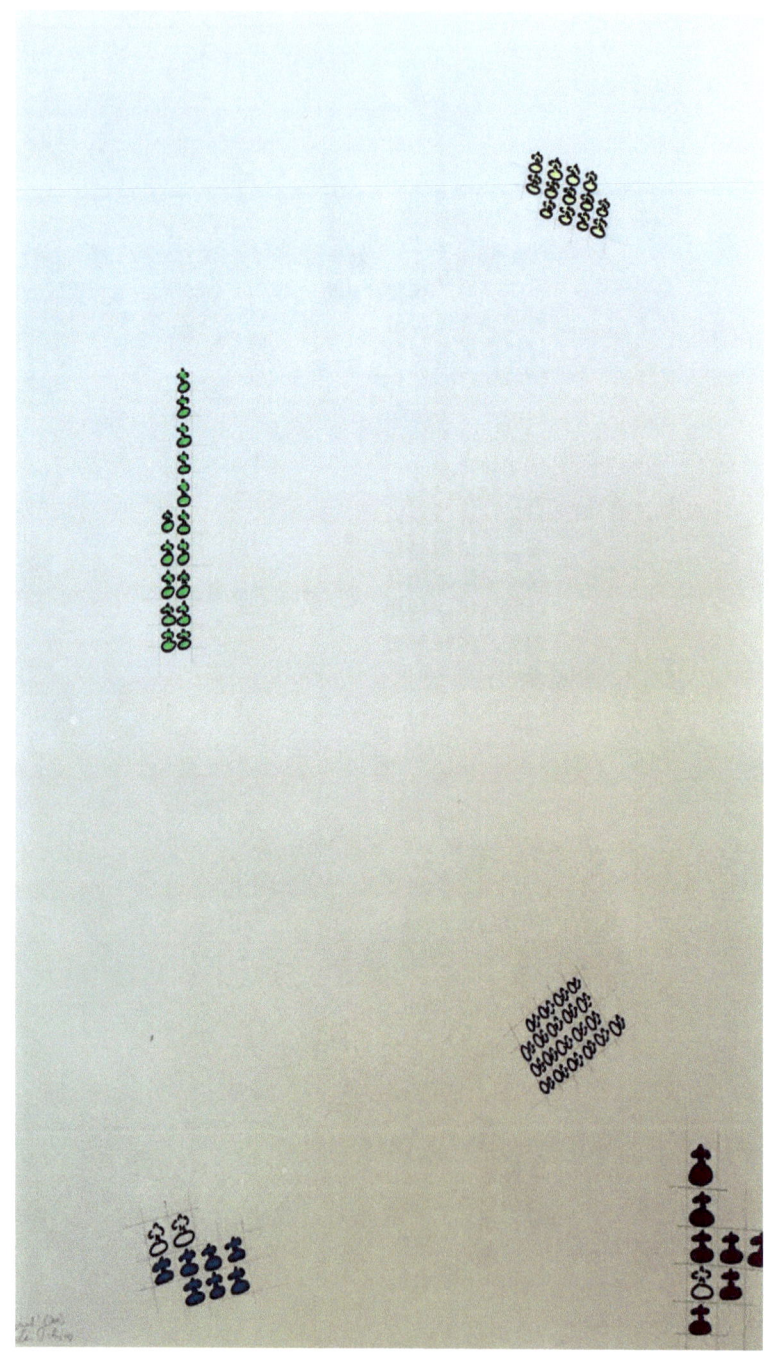

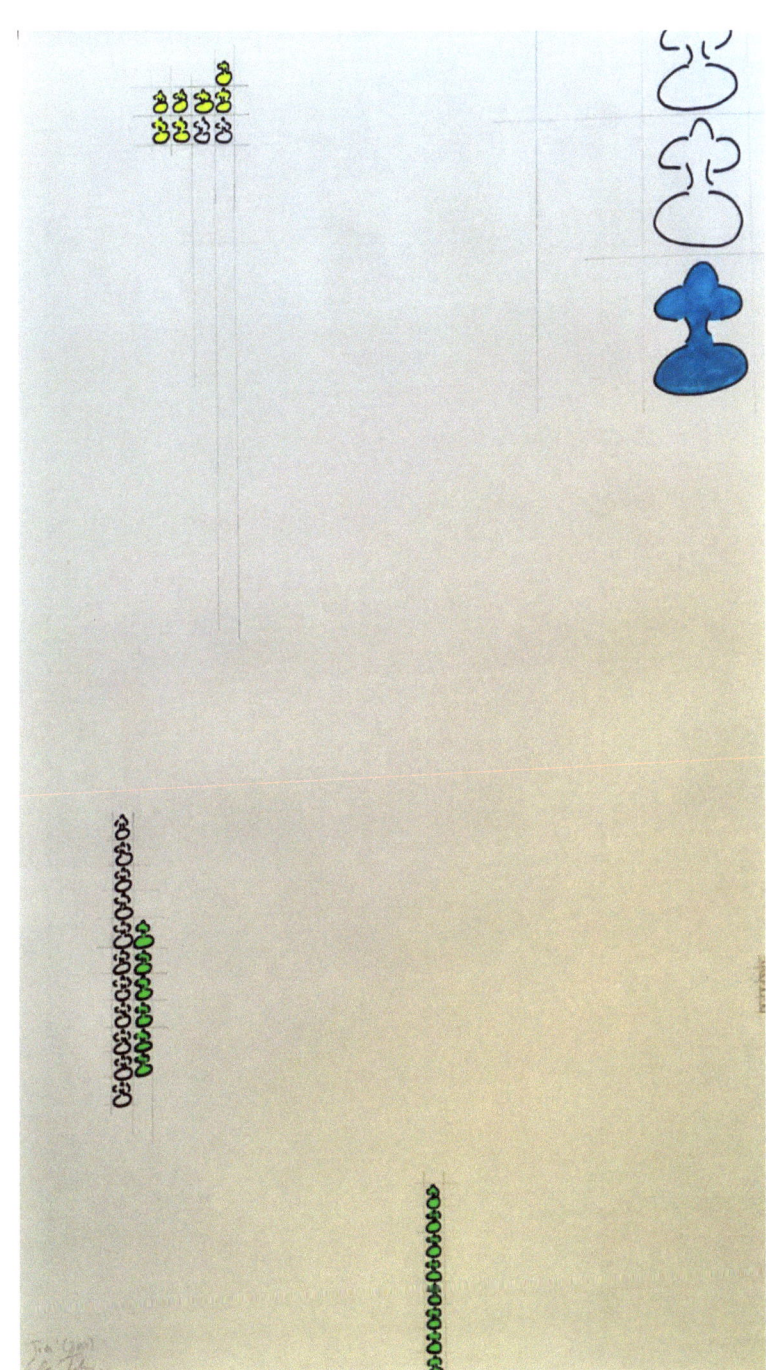

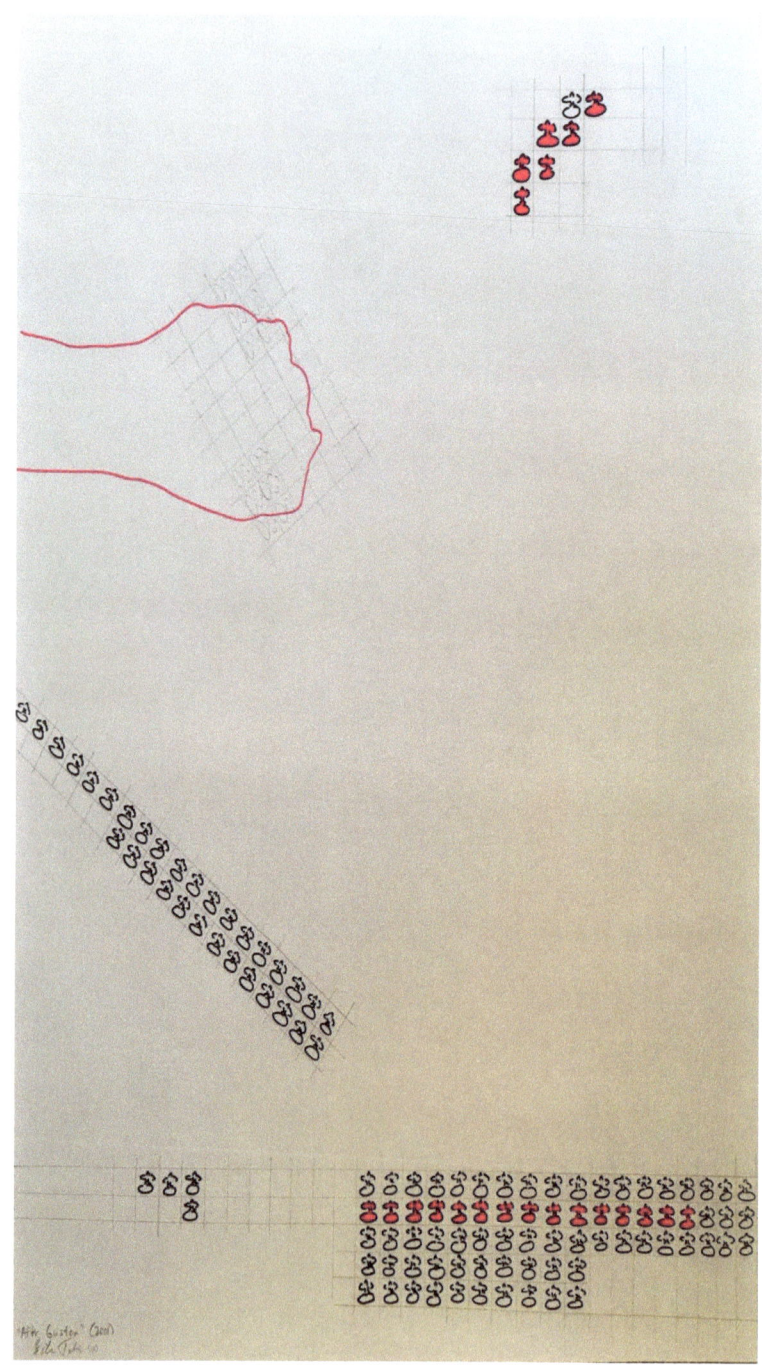

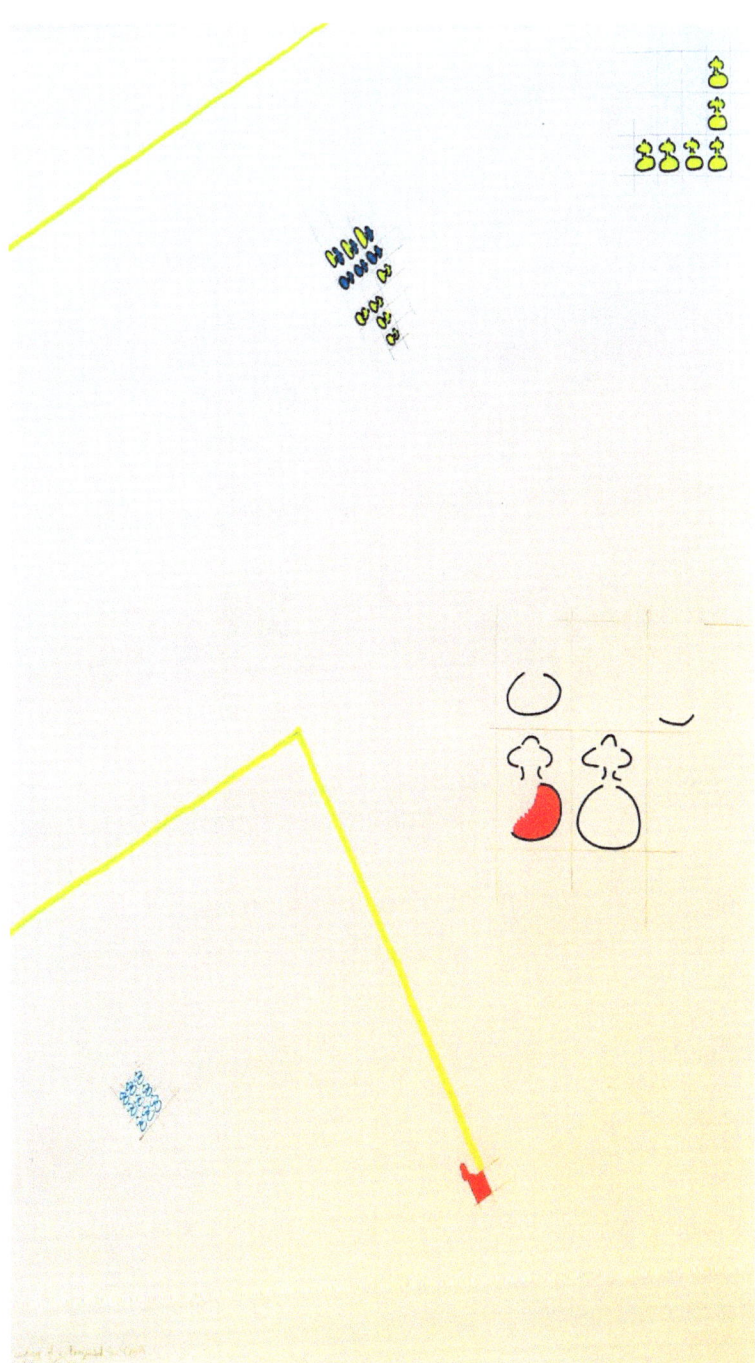

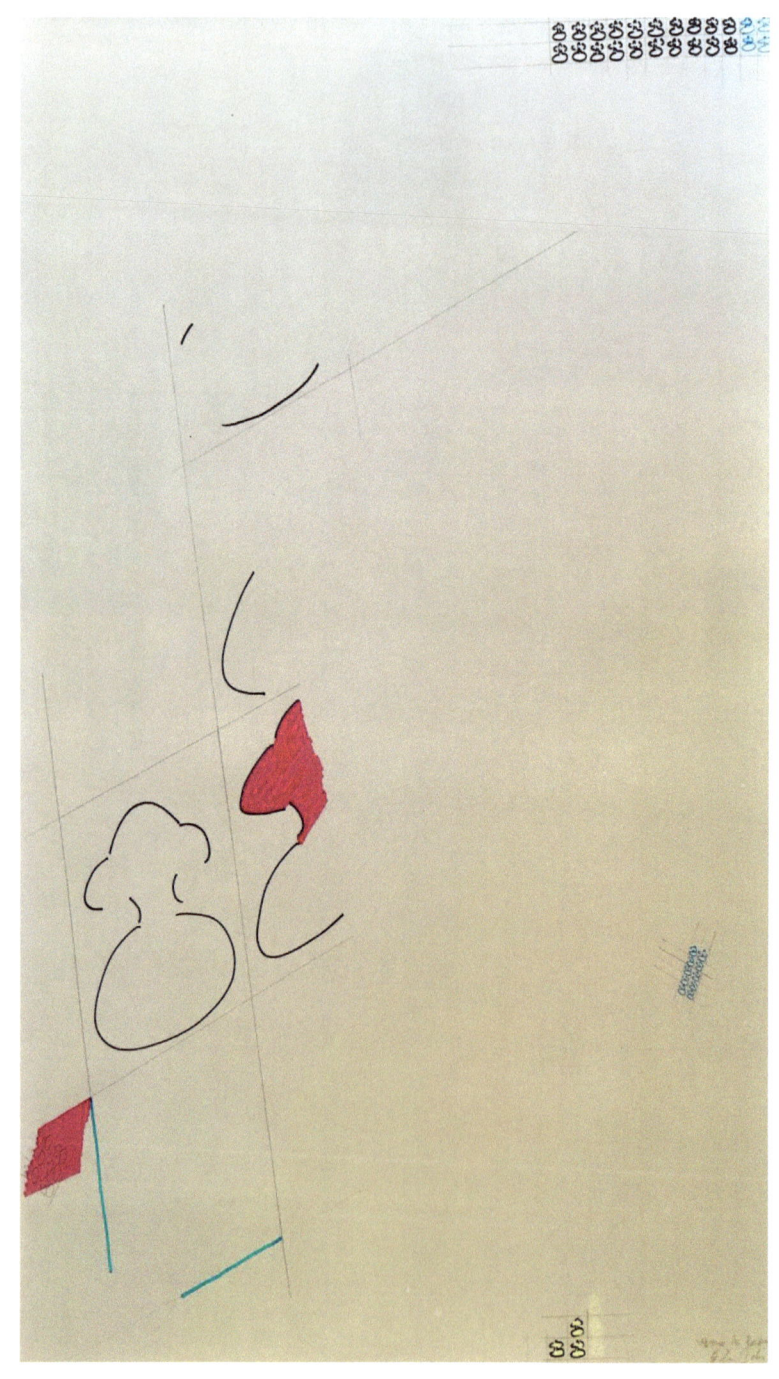

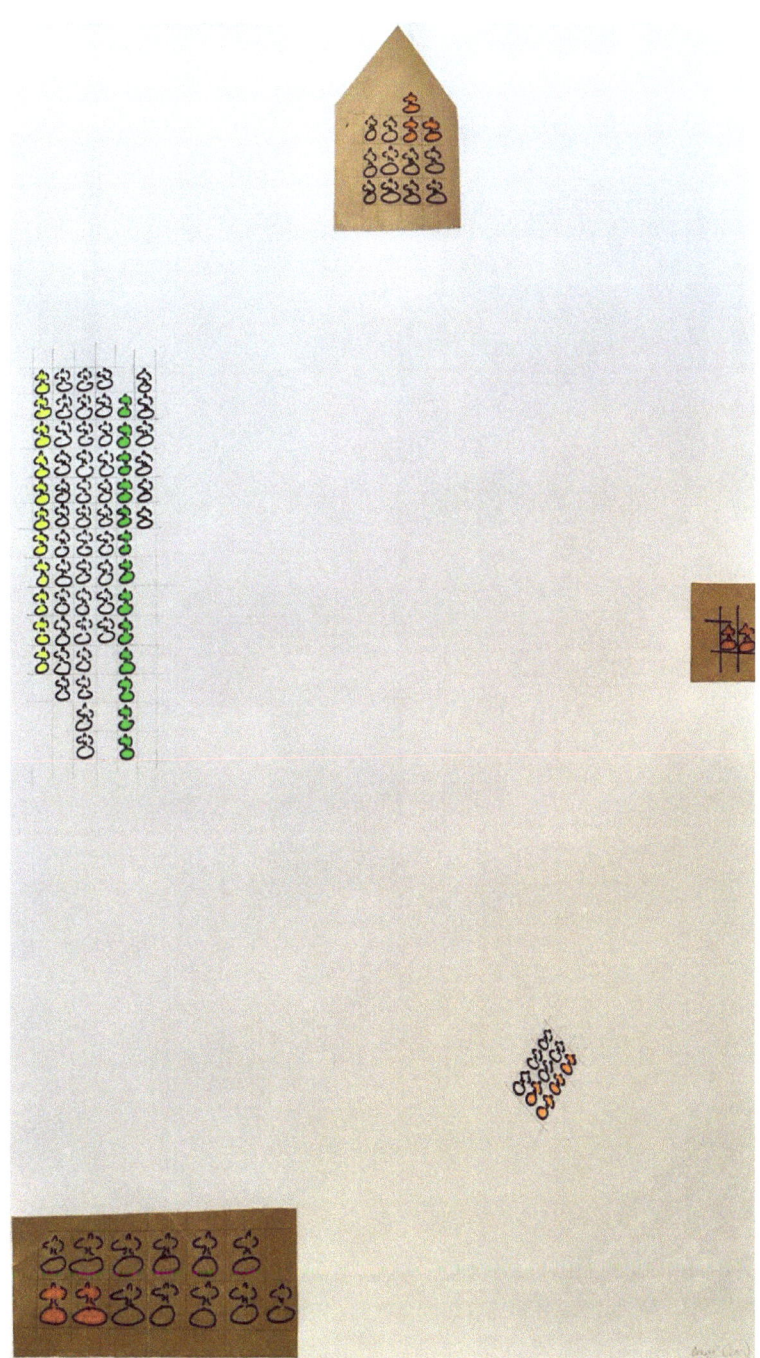

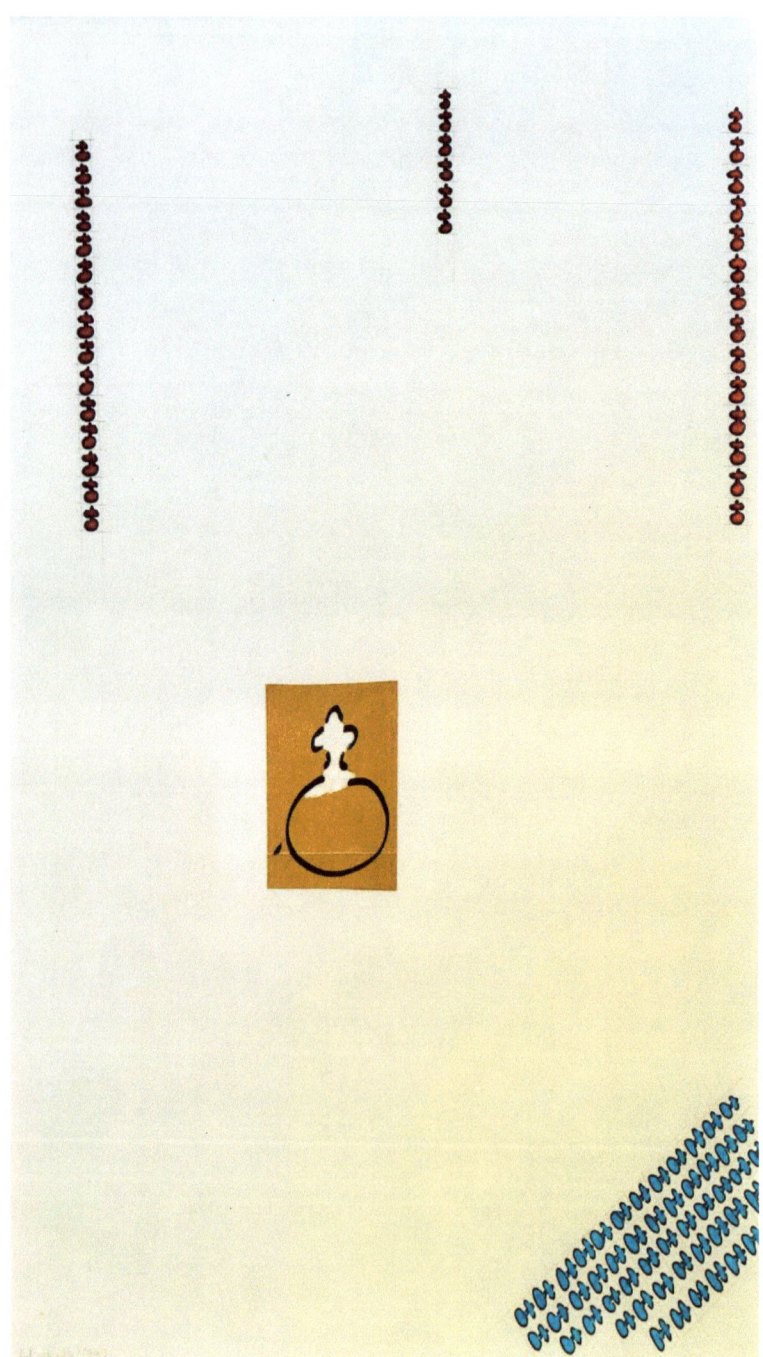

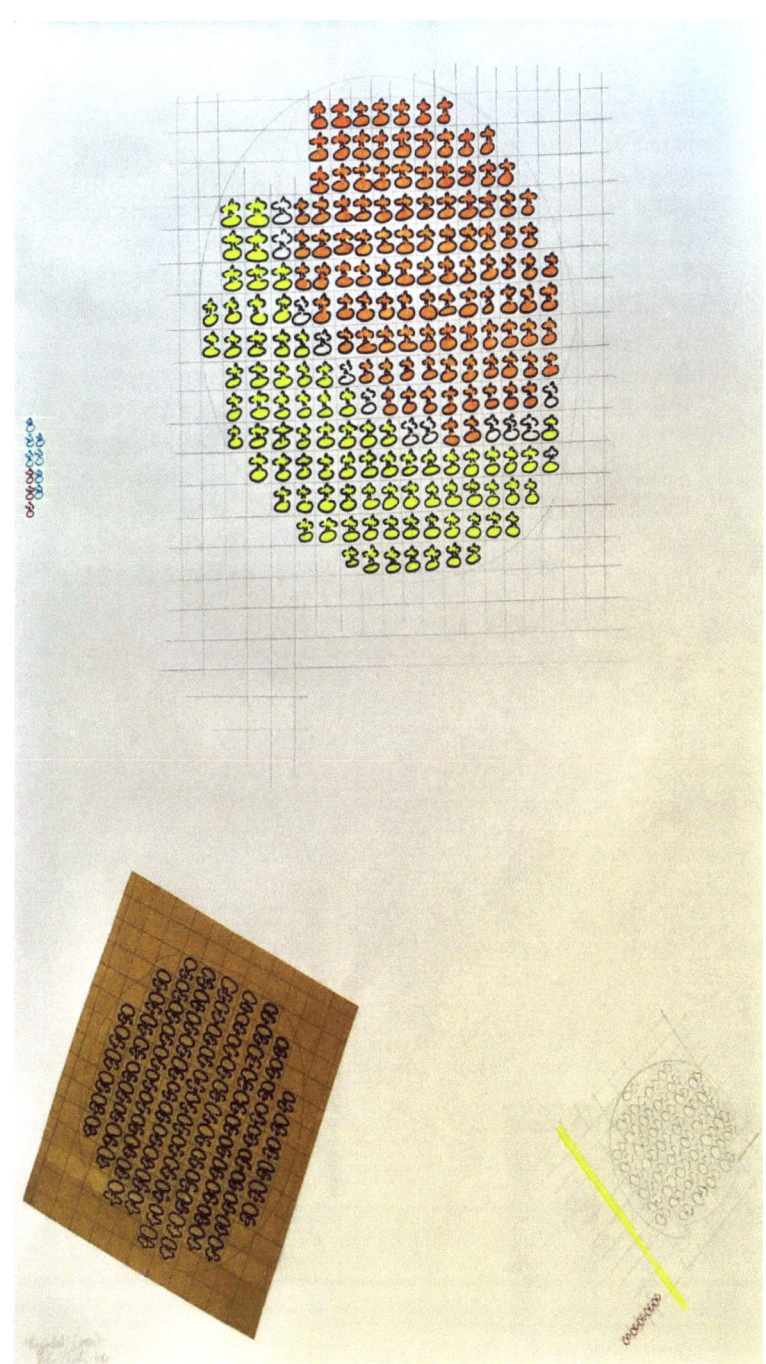

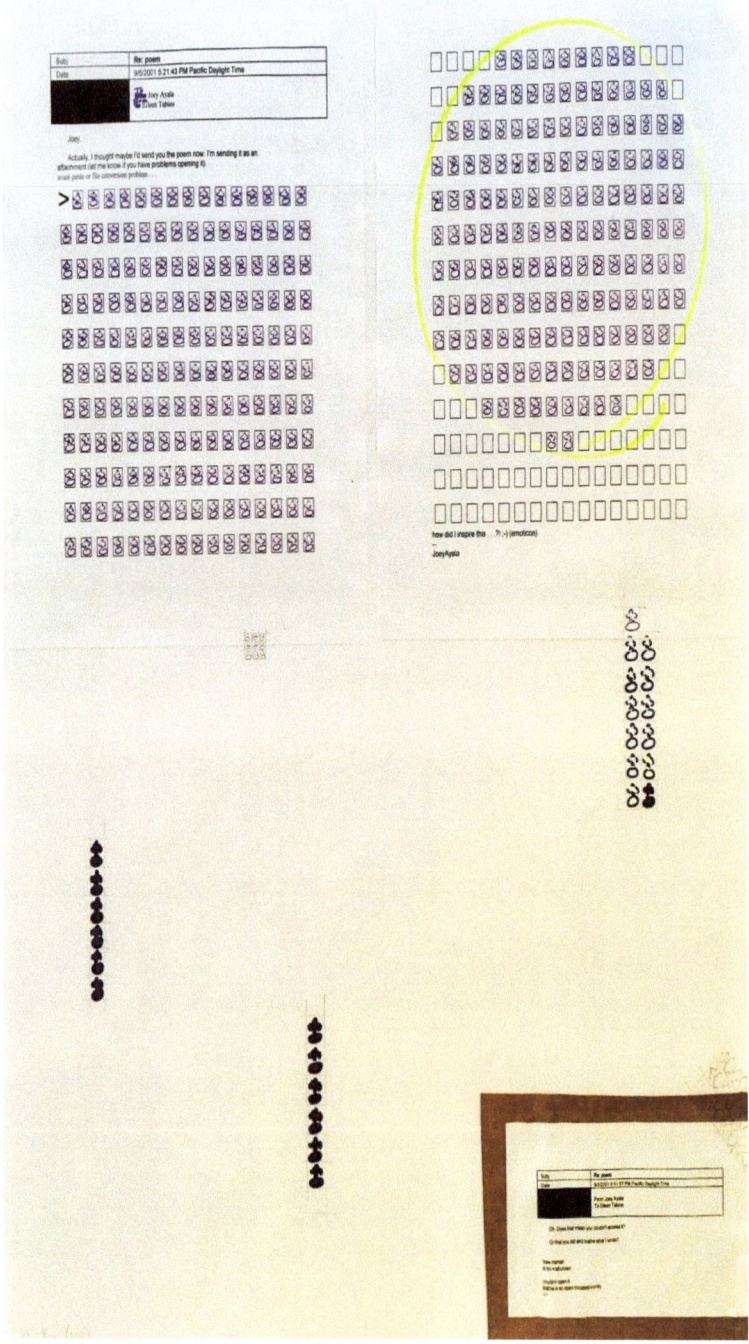

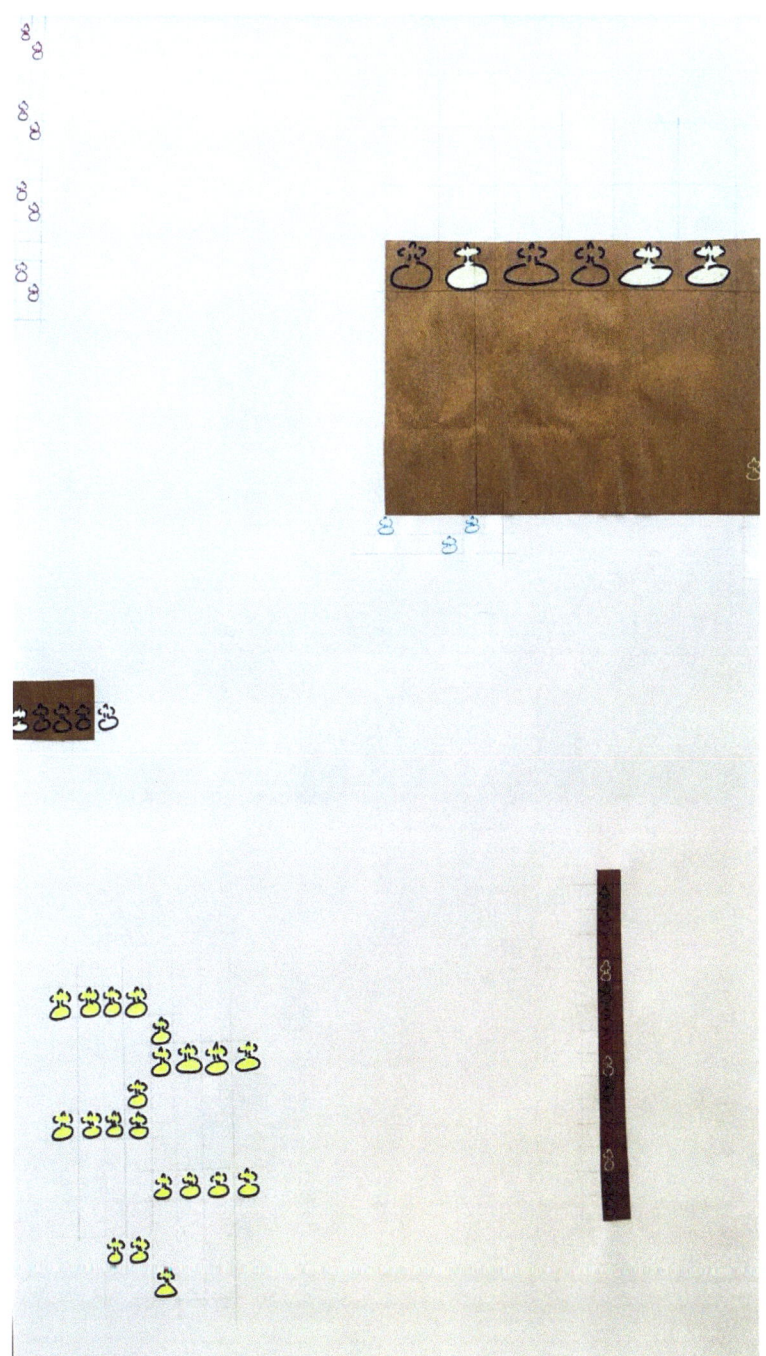

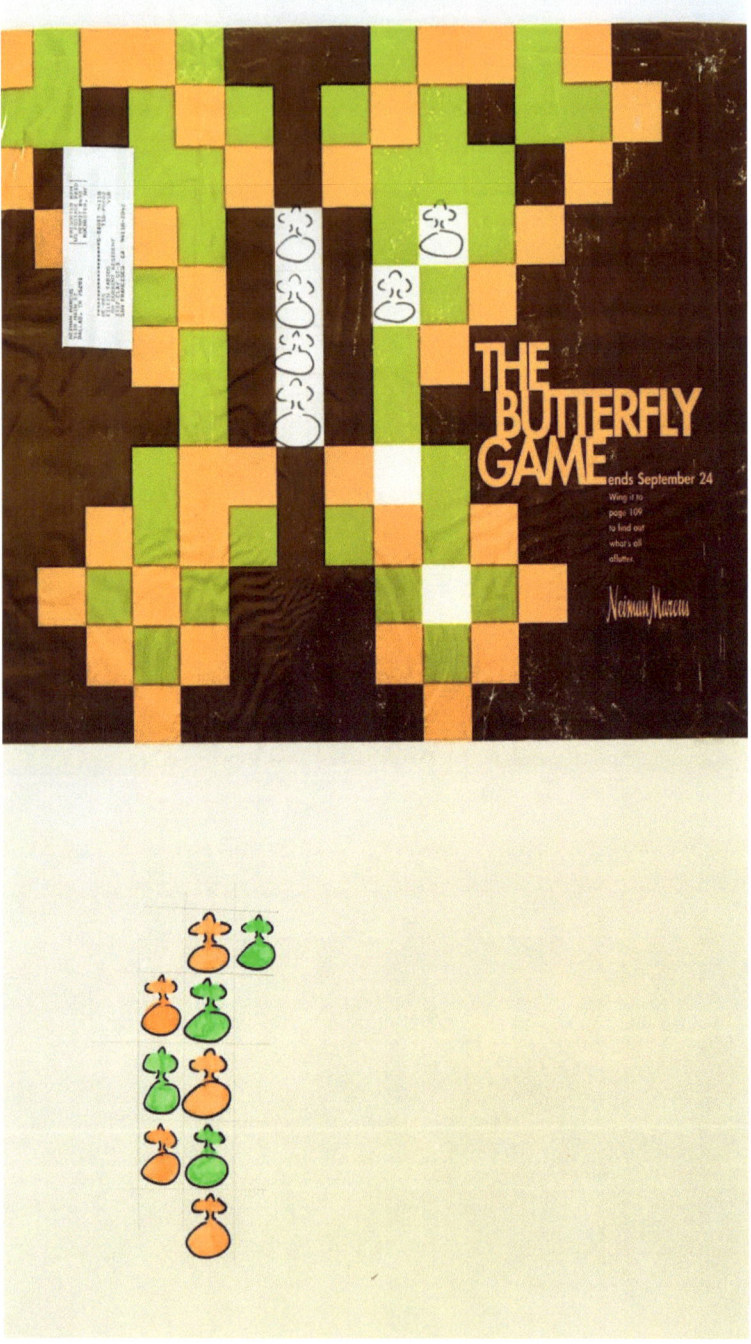

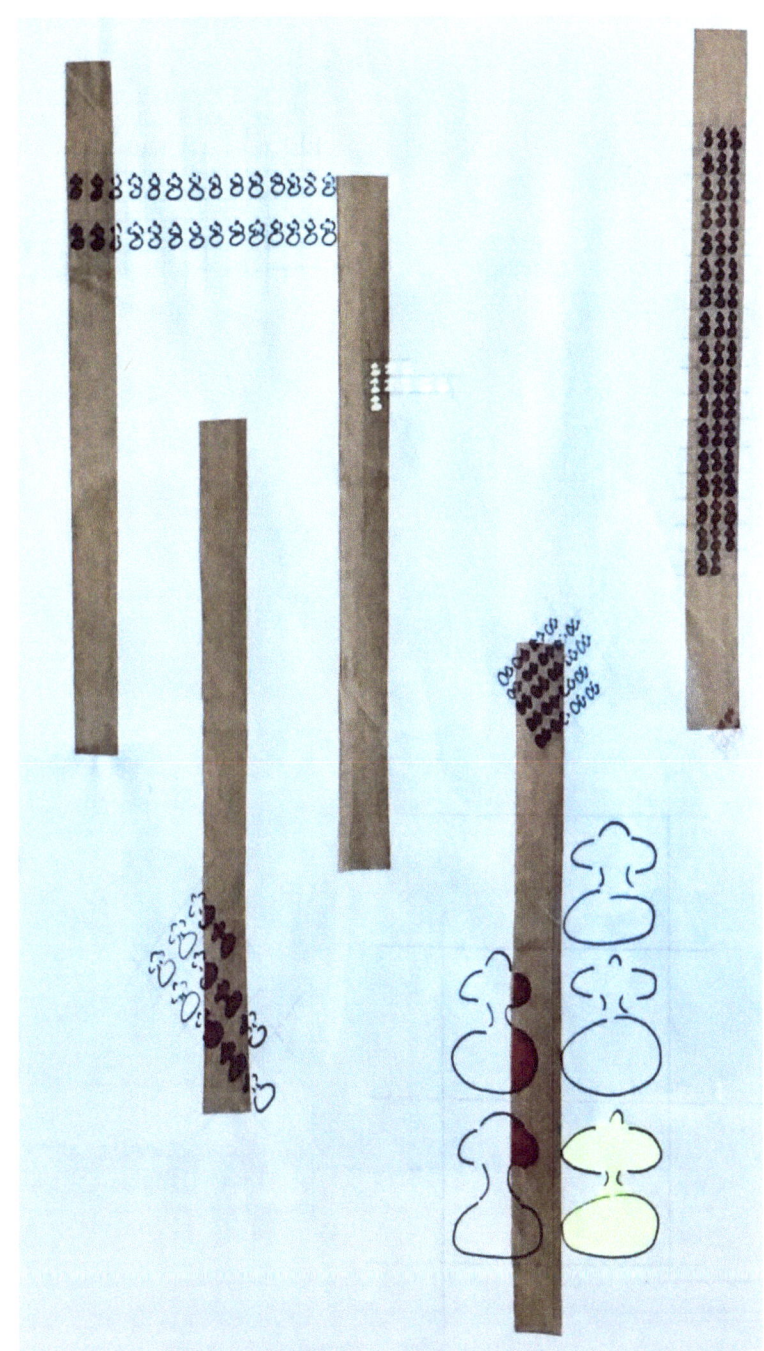

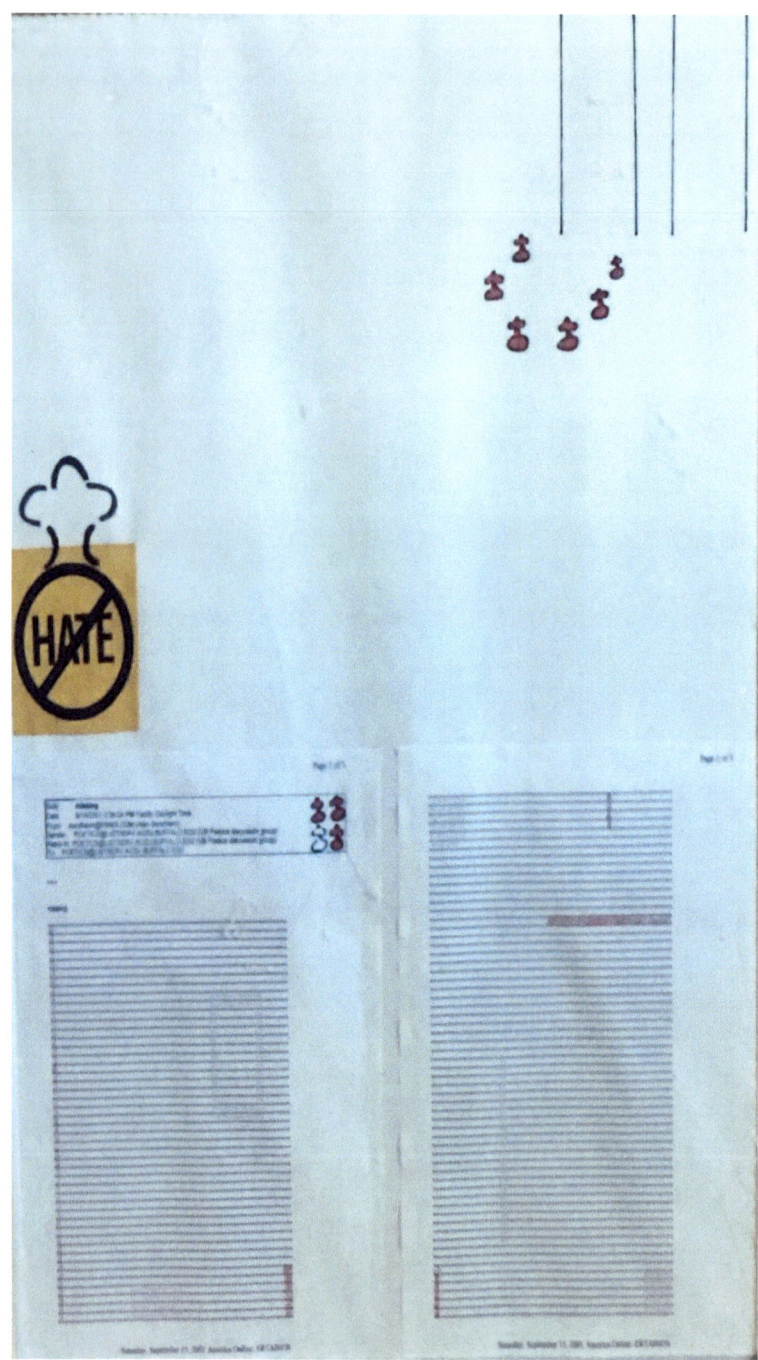

The Glitchy Mini-Folio

Note: This folio is the first publication of some of the Six Directions drawings. With an Artist Statement, this was presented through Glitchy Womyn: An anthology of women glitching in 2022-23, *Editors Kristine Snodgrass and Karla Van Vliet (Dusie Press, 2024).*

Artist Statement

These three drawings are created through a "mark" I conceptualized to mean "diasporic Filipino poet." The mark is an image of a gourd and references certain indigenous myths that describe how the first or certain humans came out of a cracked gourd(s). In this series of drawings, my "mark" is consistently the gourd icon. For example, if I drew a horizon, I would use tiny gourd images lined up closely together to form a horizontal line.

I created this image as part of visually exploring poetry. But as I created this series of drawings, I began to appreciate drawing based on its own nature, not as a means to something else (such as making a poem). *Drawing just to draw.* As well, I became interested in drawing space, as demarcated by the contrasting visibility of my gourd-based marks. I also made colored drawings as stand-alone works so that I could focus on color which I began introducing into my works.

With hindsight, this all seems fitting: by coming to relate to drawing based on drawing's own nature, I took on a more respectful approach to the media. I ended up paying more direct attention to the nature of drawing itself—to seeing drawing for itself rather than as a tool for another interest. If you wish to respect someone or something, it's best to see them for what they are rather than through your own biases or preconceptions. This whole process made me respect—then more appreciate—drawing as its own form. It's an appropriate result: respect for the multiple facets of the world—whether it's for other cultures or for the nature of physical material—is an integral concept underlying my poetry.

This project concluded with the "glitch" of me turning away from my intention to explore poetic identity and instead focus on drawing, then a media new to me. I appreciate the result—poetry often concludes with a(n opening to a) new beginning.

—Eileen R. Tabios

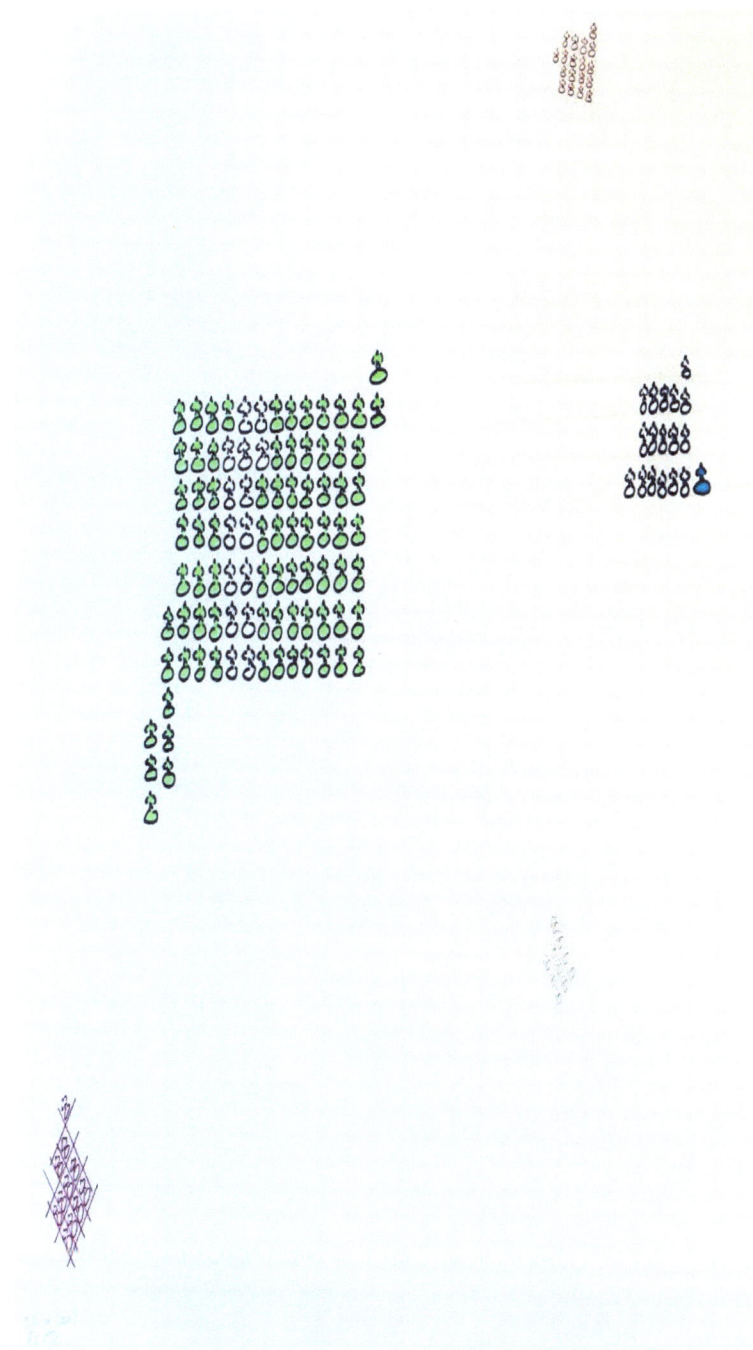

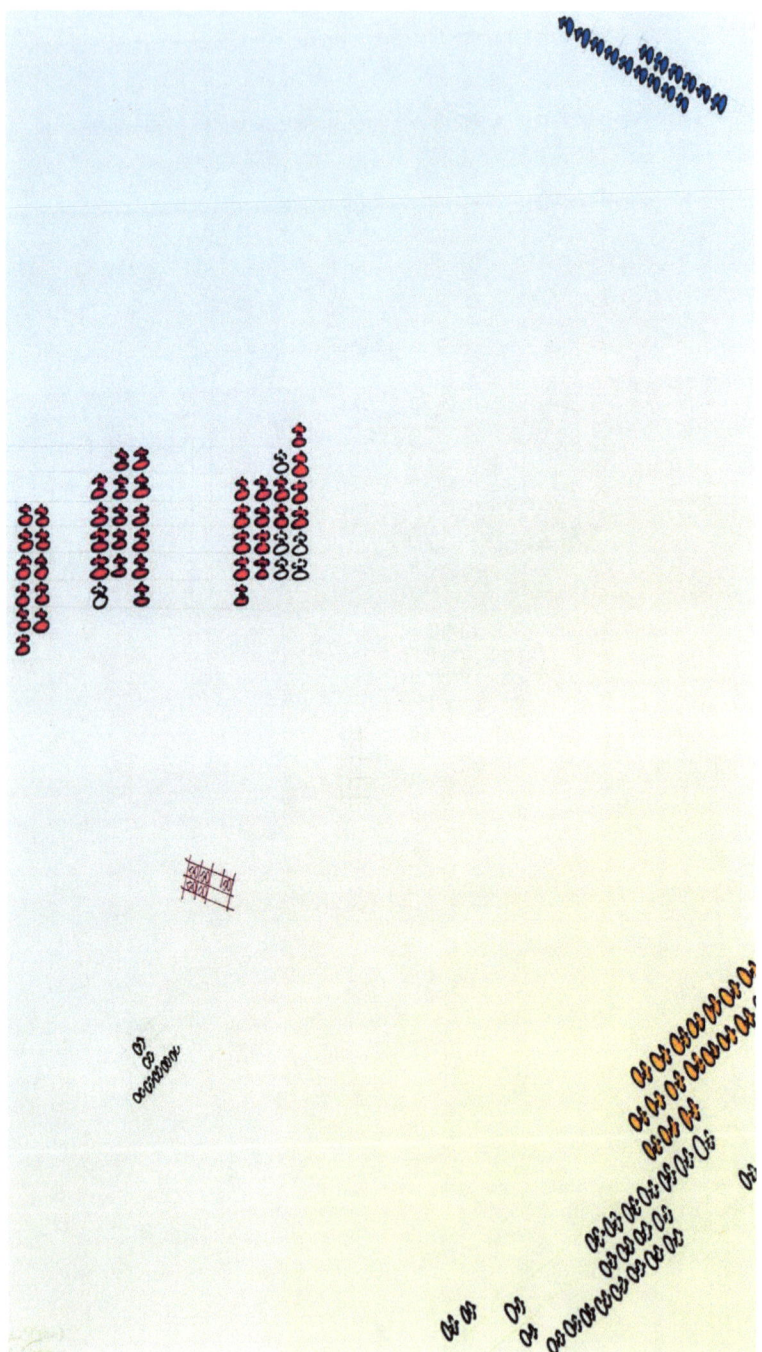

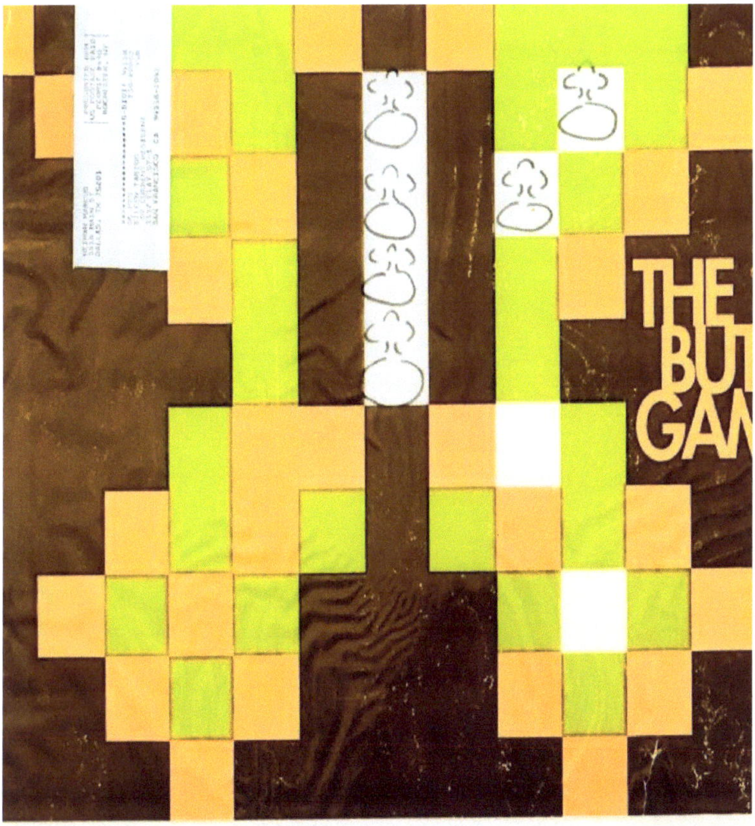

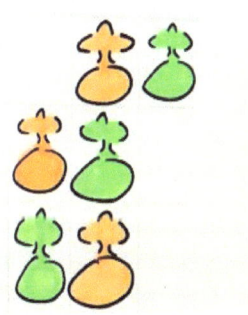

***Selected Poems From
The Six Directions***

Dear One

(i)

Beauty is reasonable

Fear
is a
Loss

Shall we wish for
what we have made

Desire
should never be
consigned

Dear One—
       Fervently,
I believe in
the ancient fisherman's motto:
"Allah does not subtract
from the allotted time of man
the hours spent fishing."

V I V I D
is
subjective

Dear One—
      I have become the sum
of a series of small
tactical errors—
regretfully, I depart
for Auckland

(ii)

Perhaps
at the equestrian center…

Shall we consider
grounding the border
with abrashed aubergine

It's not
what you can get
every day

Consider Tortola,
Virgin Gorda—
the 60-plus British Virgin Islands

Dear One—
      I saw the Bengal Tiger
mimic a helicopter's dance

A L O H A
means
"a fifth night free
plus a daily buffet breakfast for two

(iii)

The
Stark
Touch

Dear One—
          When luxury is
a necessity, recall
the hidden bones of the Villa D'Este

Forever
is
a
Theory

(iv)

Lineage seduces

A Five-Star Mobil Home
(courtesy of the Carlyle)

Manolo Blahnik's elegy for crocodiles

Dear One—
      It's not just a new car
It's the momentary immortality

The World Is Yours

(i)

when even Bulgarians
pay dividends

when Eastern Europe
restores housing

when the Future remains
"rooted in the past"

(ii)

Who shall defeat
the giants playing golf
while *white* proxy cards
get hijacked
by a coke bottler
eliminating 2,000 jobs

The Internet implodes
from calls for the next generation
while Russian cartographers
attack Vanitas Software

Sap.com rushes
its employee orientations
as the "new economy"
becomes the "new New Economy"

Offstage from a dream
a deep voice proclaims
"Soon we will be writing
to formally ask for your support"

How to turn information
into cash
while empowering executives
to promote smart energy management

when "Mutual Funds"
is clearly an oxymoron

when Merrill Lynch's growth funds
post negative yields, year-to-date

when pork bellies slump
from weakened futures

Must Tupperware return
to the headlines

Katherine Graham
is dead

Mike Saltzeim no longer spins
Coney Island's carousel

through sunlit summers, ice-cold
winters and "lurching changes"
roiling "the amusement trade"—
Mike Saltzeim's heart has failed.

(iii)

Today, in San Antonio and Fresno,
the temperature topped 100 degrees

Baseball is demeaned
by calls to broaden the strike zone

Mark Wohlers allowed nine hits
and four walks within 5 innings

Nor are encores easy
at the British Open

(iv)

The Minnesota Twins will swallow
$5 million for Joe Mauer

The world is yours
through a laptop:
computers
　　　　never
　　　　　　crash
from yearning
for *Home*

A pathologist embodies logic
by becoming a champion marathoner

At Bryant Park: Perfect Form
—New York City

(i)

Perfect
Form

Is

Occurring
From

Ground

Zero
When

Absence

Enables
Play

(ii)

The
Miniature

Environments

Created
For

And

Ultimately
Destroyed

Within

Action
Movies

Find

A
Mirror

In

Chris
Burden's

Large

"dimness.
And"

(iii)

I

Left
L.A.

To

Make
Love

With

You
At

The

Bryant Park

Hotel

In
N.Y.C.

(iv)

Dusk

Did
Not

Diminish

Our

Bryant Park

Conversations

(v)

I
Dry

Your

Pink
Toes

With

My
Hair

(vi)

Her

*Flawless
Level*

Of

*Technical
Expertise*

Appropriately

And

Deliberately

Decisive:

The
Work

Looks

Like
A

Perfect
Fake

(vii)

Kneeling

I
Submit

For

Your
Pleasure

Over

Perfect
Forms

(vii)

Oh

Bryant Park!

(ix)

Despite

An
Impassive

Face

Your
Lips

Sweetly

Formed
"Yes"

(x)

Oh

Bryant Park!

Oh

Perfect
Form!

Wine Tasting Notes

An expanding idea

shifts scale to larger than life

imagery from pictorial to abstraction

tone from silent to aggressive

    "yet in each there is a common commitment"

Tactile pleasures

suggest a world worth experiencing

by celebrating the perplexities

of knowing

Experience art

through self-encounter

"This is not a vase"

    "This is not a river"

Subjectivity is

the plankton beneath the wave

radiating from green into gold

with the onset of wet sunlight

From The Gray Monster In A Yellow Taxi

I desire most
when it rains

      :

How can one
label history
an "absence"

As if dissonance
can ever be "subtle"

Like the absence of
yellow taxis during days of gray water

Can fantasy
not be poignant

Does not reality
always leave
us wanting more

Antarctica keens
the Siren Song
of an unnamed woman
longing to be overcome
by an avalanche
not made of snow

More poets should
experiment with

"foundational questioning"

To rhapsodize over
"The River of Heaven"

Otherwise Pain
becomes
"our very own lack of pain"

While death persists
as a premature topic

The tale of the "Dirty War"
in Argentina (1976-1983)
is one of language
because all leftists
left Buenos Aires

This does not signify
a painting is
a blank canvas

Ask any Russian
at a funeral party

Fire is always
"destruction"—
do not believe
the one who says otherwise
with an expertise
claimed through a label:
"P O E T"

To be accurate, define
Fire as Diane di Prima

aborting a child
because the man she loved
"willed it so"

We choose
what we name

We choose those "karmic traces"

Dream =/= Democracy

Yes, look back
Look Back
The Bible is only a book

Sometimes we have nothing
to give
but still give—
this could be confidence
This could be religion

This could be Blissful Ignorance

This could be orgasm

This could be, or Not

This could be an excuse
one gets away with
by serving up certain words
like "paradox"

Or "transcendence"

Or "archetype"

Or ascribing the role of creator
to a lettuce spinner's
whirlpool of paper slips
manufactured by the Chinese:
> e.g. a lottery poem
> birthed through lines
> that spilled
> between plastic cracks

This issue of *Rain Taxi* ends
with a non-coincidence:
"Catastrophe Theory"—
evolution through mutations
conflagrated by
failures to understand

Thus, monsters also hope

Look back
Look Back
The Bible is only a book—
I am still here

And I am breathing

I Breathe

For Charles Henri Ford

The glowworm
turns professorial
when stars hide

A white azalea
quiets the shade
into a girl

The girl loves marble
enough to freeze
into a swoon

While ascending from trellis jail
the jasmine's skin
comes to miror the sky

From a factory
questionable grit escapes
within the cover of gray haze

You want to live
You live to want
As if to anguish is to feel

Tongue the cracks
to glue together
fragments of a stolen sun

Revel
in the claw marks
forking a cheek

Oh, Poet
preening at the labyrinth --
unlatch that gate

You, there
with blue veins
crackling transparent membrane

Afterword:

Poems From The Six Directions

The Six Directions project began with making mixed-media sculptures, a process that eventually led to drawings. The sculptures themselves created matching poems. The following Notes present some background to some of the poems.

<u>At Bryant Park: Perfect Form</u>

The poem began initially through a response to the early sections of the article "Shiny Happy People: Art and Special Effects" by Jennifer Cooper in *New Art Examiner*, July/August 2001. The article discusses the influence of Hollywood's special-effects industry on the contemporary sculpture created in urban Southern California; it begins with the line, "This is a story about perfect forms." Featured with the article is a tiny illustration, a reproduction of John McCracken's sculpture "Live It Up in Lilac (1967)." Made from Polyester resin, fiberglass, plywood, the sculpture is a rectangular white board standing up against a wall. I thought the image to be perfect for my sculpting a poem because the white surface of the rectangle evokes a page. Despite its scale of 104" x 18" x 3", the reproduction is tiny and so I thought to create a poem by envisioning either one or two words that would be lettered at the bottom of the image.

Some of the poem's words respond deliberately to some of the text in the article, e.g. Section (ii) stems from the statement, "...the tropes and syntax of the movie and entertainment business have become inseparable from those of certain West Coast art practices. <u>For example, the miniaturized environments created for and ultimately destroyed within action movies find a mirror in Chris Burden's large-scale dioramas</u>." And Section (vi) stems from the statement, "The objects that comprise Jennifer Pastor's 'Four Seasons' from 1997 are hyper-realistic but symbolic representations of the different times of the year. Rendered in plastic and other artificial materials, they look like fantasy objets for a movie set as they disrupt the viewer's cognizance of both scale and authenticity....<u>The flawless level of Pastor's technical execution is decisive. Her work looks like a good fake</u>." *[Underlines are the author's.]*

However, the poem also became a fictionalized narrative about something that could have occurred in Bryant Park Hotel where I stayed during a July 8-15, 2001 visit to New York City. I thought of Bryant Park because I still had my hotel room key, whose 2 ¾" x 8 ½" scale made me think that it could be the perfect book cover to this poem written on the 2" x 5 ½" reproductions of McCracken's sculpture.

*

Dear One

Each stanza in the poem was inspired by an image and/or text in the April 2000 *TOWN & COUNTRY* magazine, as featured here in the same order as the stanzas:

1) Baccarat ad with the statement: "Beauty has its reasons."
2) Fireman's Fund ad entitled "Fear of Losing"
3) Alitalia ad with the phrase "Let's make a wish"

4) Phillips International Auctioneers & Valuers ad
5) "Why I Fish," an article by David Halberstam
6) MacKenzie-Childs, Ltd. ad with the word "VIVID"
7) As one of the illustrations for "Sail Away" by Anthony Barzilay Freund, an article covering the Louis Vuitton Cup Challenge in New Zealand, a photo taken by Luca Trovato with the caption: "The New York Yacht Club's Team Young America, barely recovered from their boat's splitting in half during the second round of racing, subsequently suffered a series of small tactical errors that added up to their early departure from Auckland."
8) Las Campanas Santa Fe ad with the phrase "What's keeping you from owning a home with a world-class equestrian center in your backyard?"
9) Doris Leslie Blau Ltd. Ad featuring a carpet with the caption: "A late 19th century Persian Sultanabad carpet measuring 15'3" x 11'8" with a pale rust ground on which large floral devices are asymmetrically placed giving a strong feeling of the Arts and Crafts influence. Teal blue, pale yellow, apricot olive green and an abundant amount of banana adds to the vitality and warmth of the piece. The ground of the major border is a beautifully abrashed aubergine on which large scale devices freely flow."
10) BMW ad with the phrase "It's not a feeling you can get every day."
11) The British Virgin Islands ad
12) *Town & Country*'s Contributors page, including notes on photographer Luca Trovato who said, "I had never shot from a helicopter before. It offered an amazing view of an extremely graceful dance" as well as deputy editor John Cantrell who said about his trip through India and Nepal that he and nine

other animal lovers spent several days searching the lush wilderness before finally catching a single glimpse of the elusive and endangered Bengal tiger.
13) The Ritz-Carlton Kapalua ad that includes the phrase "Aloha is a word famous for its many meanings"
14) Stark Carpet ad that includes the phrase "With every step, the Stark Touch"
15) Loro Piana ad with the phrase "When Luxury is a Necessity"
16) De Beers ad with the slogan "A Diamond Is Forever"
17) Radisson Seven Seas Cruises ad with the proclamation: "And what a show-stopper she'll be, if her lineage is any indication. The first ship ever to offer all ocean-view suites with private balconies, the ultra-spacious Seven Seas Mariner promises to make a name for herself while still an infant."
18) The Carlyle ad with the phrase "A Mobil Five-Star Hotel For Over A Quarter Of A Century"
19) Bergdorf Goodman ad with a photo of Manolo Blahnik shoes
20) Infiniti I30 ad with the phrase "Introducing the all-new Inifiniti I30./ It's not just a new car./ It's all the best thinking."

*

From The Grey Monster In A Yellow Taxi
I.   Appropriated Words

Most of the stanzas reflect the influence of found text within the issue of *Rain Taxi*, Vol. 6, No. 2, Summer 2001. In addition, the phrase "Whose Heart is A Rose Tattoo" was included in the title to reflect the title of

John Yau's book entitled "My Heart Is That Eternal Rose Tattoo" (which the author was reading while the poem was being sculpted). From *Rain Taxi*, the poem's references are:

Stanza No.	*Rain Taxi* Found Text
1	Magazine Cover with "Rain Taxi"
2	"Ghost Stories," Alan Gilbert's review of Renee Gladman's *JUICE* that begins "The writing of history's absence is like a ghost story…"
3	Julie Madsen's review of Patricia Wilcox's *SHAPED NOTES* whose first paragraph ends with "…to cause a dissonance that subtly vexes the reader."
5	Alan DeNiro's review of Jonathan Carroll's *THE WOODEN SEA* that ends with the lines, "…but at the same time only begins to hint at the deep emotional poignancies that are drawn out through Carroll's use of the fantastic."
6	Brian Evenson's review of Patrick Ehlen's *FRANTZ FANON* that includes the phrase, "There are moments in Frantz Fanon which leave one wanting more though this says as much about the limitations (and perhaps strengths) of the short biography…"
7	Peter Ritter's review of John Long's *MOUNTAINS OF MADNESS*, about the exploration of Antarctica.
8	"Language As Felt," Eric Lorberer's interview with Alice Fulton who, at one point, says, "Science appeals to me

73

because it offers truly fresh metaphors, and it encourages foundational questioning."

9   A Carnegie Mellon advertisement that mentions Garrett Hongo's book *THE RIVER OF HEAVEN* (which presents a significantly different approach to poetry than Alice Fulton's – a juxtaposition that made me consider the way the personal still underpins a language-based approach to poetry

10 John Olson's review of Christopher Reiner's *PAIN* that ends with the statement, "Our real pain is our very lack of pain."

12 Mary Sarko's review of Ricardo Piglia's *THE ABSENT CITY* that begins, "During Argentina's Dirty War (1976-1983), many writers on the political left chose to leave the country."

14 Mention of the Russian author Ludmila Ulitskaya's book entitled *THE FUNERAL PARTY*

15 Rebecca Weaver's review of Anne Waldman's audio, *ALCHEMICAL ELEGY* which quotes from one of Waldman's poems: "May you be inside each other / traveling through each others bodies / like this fire...is not destruction."

16 In Chris Fischbach's review of Diane Prima's *RECOLLECTIONS OF MY LIFE AS A WOMAN*, the reviewed book is excerpted to depict di Prima's recollection: "Since Roi didn't want the child, I felt that if I Loved him, it was incumbent on me to

have an abortion no matter what I was feeling. To show the extent of my love by doing what I felt in fact was wrong. To commit what for me was tantamount to a crime, simply because the man I loved willed it so. And I would take the blame, the consequences, the blood on my hands. And not say anything about it."

18   Mention of Eliot Weinberger's book entitled *KARMIC TRACES*

19   Mention of Mark Ford's book entitled *RAYMOND ROUSSEL AND THE REPUBLIC OF DREAMS*

23   Mention of Nin Andrews' book entitled *THE BOOK OF ORGASMS*

28   Eric Lorberer's review of Clayton Ashleman's *ERRATICS* which describes how "Eshleman typed 'the lines I wanted to do something with' on separate slips of paper and spun them in a lettuce dryer'."

29   Jason Picone's article, "Practicing Catastrophe in the work of Nicholas Mosley"

In addition, stanza 13 reflects the image of David Klamen's "Untitled (2000)," a series of rectangular watercolors on paper. The first draft was written on the margins of a reproduction of Klamen's work.

II.   Poem

I don't always write poems to say something. I write poems to see/hear what it is the poems want to say. At the beginning of creating this work, I had been mulling over the image of a series of white-gray rectangular watercolors "Untitled (2000)" by David Klamen. There are 90 watercolors that together create a hanging installation; as I looked at the rectangles and squares, they seemed to me to denote emptiness—they were like pages all awaiting (my) inscription. I began writing the poem by leafing through an issue of *Rain Taxi* for text that I could use to fill in the squares. I didn't, however, wish to relate a stanza/line/word to each individual square as I felt I already had done this approach in a prior poem-sculpture ("At Bryant Park: Perfect Form"). So I just continued writing the poem wherever *Rain Taxi's* words took me.

After writing the poem, I added the subtitle "a.k.a. "*Rain Taxi*, Vol. 6, No. 2, Summer 2001 In the Voice of Lot's Wife" because I recalled the fate of Lot's wife from the phrases "Look back" as well as "The Bible is only a book." While I didn't realize it during the actual writing process, Lot's wife was speaking between the lines of – as well as through the words in – *Rain Taxi*." I thought the presence of her voice to be logical given how she appropriated the writers as well as reviewed authors within the magazine which specializes in book reviews and author interviews. When, in the Biblical story, she was frozen, she was also silenced. I also didn't wish to join the conspiracy to look at Lot's wife with disdain because *SHE WANTED TO SEE*.

Inexplicably, I then decided to do a Yahoo search on "Lot's Wife." I say "inexplicably" as I didn't know what caused me to look for Lot's Wife in the internet—perhaps for her actual name besides the tag "Lot's wife"? There was only one site found for "Lot's Wife." It was a poem written by Anna Akhmatova. How marvelously synchronistic! For the poem incorporates the lines: "This does not signify/ a painting is a blank canvas// Ask any Russian/ at a funeral party". On the site featuring Anna's face that I now ascribe to bearing the features of Lot's Wife, there also was reference to another site under the heading ""To Go Its Way In Tears: Poems of Grief." Grief certainly seemed to be relevant, and I went to that site. And at that site, Anna is featured again with a poem she had written—*during a funeral party!* From her poem "In Memory of M.B." are these lines:

> Here is my gift, not roses on your grave,
> not sticks of burning incense....//
>
> Now you're gone, and nobody says a word
> about your troubled and exalted life.
> Only my voice, like a flute, will mourn
> at your dumb funeral feast.

Thus, Anna seemed to want me to write a poem as a "gift" for Lot's Wife to prevent no one saying a word about her "troubled and exalted life."

Following these revelations from the Internet, I was moved—it was as if someone took my hand to guide me to—go to the kitchen. There, in one of the cupboards, I found the salt container. I took off the label from the salt container as I felt that it should be incorporated in the poem-sculpture. At the time, I kept hearing a phrase run through my mind like an unwounding tape: "salt unbound, salt unbound, salt unbound..." As in: desalinize Lot's frozen statue and make her live again. The salt label became the "book cover." I believe that the notion I sensed of an unwounding tape also facilitated my next idea to create

77

a scroll of pages "covered" by the salt-related cover and bound with a ribbon once used for a corporate gift by Paul Hastings. Paul Hastings is an appropriate moniker as they are a law firm and, in this day and age, lawyers are used for "due diligence" research, for recovery purposes, for regress. Later, as I first bound the scroll with the Paul Hastings "found" ribbon, I would realize its aptness: because of its length, it takes time to unwind—unbound—the scroll, fitting the "salt, unbound" concept of the cover.

I would place the scroll in an ornate box that, in my mind, embodies Pandora's box. But the scroll also would include a blue-and-white figurine of a lady from Russia as well as a statue of Kwan-yin—respectively, Anna and the Goddess of Mercy. I initially envisioned the inclusion of colorful ribbons to symbolize the pleasure of a woman no longer silenced and now with a name: "Anna." Later, I would replace the ribbons with "green grass" confetti as I thought the greenery symbolized the fertility of mind, including the imagination of the Poem that would bring Lot's wife back to life.

*

The World Is Yours
Each stanza in the poem was inspired by text from each page of the C Section of the July 18, 2001 *New York Times* (which encompassed business and sports news), as featured here in the same order as the stanzas:

1) the headline "A Bet on Bulgaria Pays Dividends"
2) the sentence "Still, as Eastern Europe restores housing neglected by decades of Communism and

builds new homes for its expanding middle class, the potential is huge" (from "A Bet on Bulgaria Pays Dividends" by John Tagliabue

3) New Wachovia ad with the phrase "SunTrust is Rooted in the Past"

4) the section COMPANY NEWS, a First Union ad with the call for shareholders "to vote for the Wachovia/First Union merger by returning the white proxy card," and the headline "Coke Bottler To Eliminate 2,000 Jobs"

5) a CRM ad highlighting the advantages of the Web and the phrase "The Next Generation of CRM" and the headline "U.S. Arrests Russian Cryptographer as Copyright Violator"

6) a SAP ad with the phrase "beats sitting through employee orientation" and a Columbia Executive Management Program ad with the phrase "the new New Economy has changed the role of technology in the business world"

7) Computer Associates ad with the phrase "Soon, we will be writing to formally ask for your support at this year's annual meeting on August 29"

8) ad for USE THE NEWS by Maria Bartiromo with the claim "Shows You How To Turn Information Into Cash" and The New York Times ad with the phrase "Empowered: Smart Energy Management"

9) section MUTUAL FUNDS

10) in the section MUTUAL FUNDS, Merrill Lynch's "Growth m" fund posts a -18.4% return, YTD

11) in the section CASH PRICES, the Tuesday rice for "pork bellies 12-14 lb. Midwest av. cwt" is 98, versus 101 the prior day

12) the continuation headline "Target Will Sell Tupperware"

13) the article and headline "Katherine Graham,

Publisher Who Transformed Washington Post, is Dead at 84"

14) the obituary titled "Mike Saltzstein, 60, Coney Island's Carousel Man, Dies

15) first paragraph of the Saltzstein obituary reads "Mike Saltzstein, who for more than a quarter-century kept Coney Island's last historic carousel spinning thorugh sunlit summers, ice-old winters and lurching changes in the famed amusement area, died on July 4 in his Brooklyn apartment. He was 60."

16) The weather map shows 100+ temperatures in the San Antonio and Fresno areas

17) Dave Anderson's column entitled "The Poison Threatening The Umpires" includes the fifth paragraph that begins with "In order to diminish the overall number of pitches and thereby shorten the sometimes dreary length of a game, umpires were recently instructed by baseball officials to broaden their interpretation of the strike zone."

18) From "In-Season Additions Fail to Add A Spark" by Buster Olney, the sentences: "Mark Wohlers, the veteran right-hander acquired in a deal with the Cincinnati Reds, has allowed nine hits and four walks in four and on-third innings, compiling a 12.46 earned run average."

19) a headline "Encores Aren't Easy at the British Open"

20) in the Baseball ROUNDUP section, the report that "Joe Mauer, the top pick in June's amateur draft, agreed yesterday on most points of a contract with the Minnesota Twins that calls for a signing bonus of just over $5 million."

21) a MARATHON report that "Christine Clark, the only American woman to compete in the marathon

in the 2000 Olympics, will run in the New York City Marathon on Nov. 4.// Clark, a 37-year-old pathologist from Anchorage, joins an elite field..."
22)	a Microsoft ad proclaiming "This computer is traveling to Dubai. Unlike its owner, the computer will never be homesick."

*

Wine Tasting Notes

    The poem was written while skimming through the catalogue for David Klamen's 2000 solo exhibition at Haines Gallery, San Francisco. Referenced text or text that offered inspiration were written by David Klamen, Kathryn Hixson, David Breskin, and Hans-George Gadamer. The illustrations are taken from the reproductions of David Klamen's works in the order they appear in the catalogue. The poem was titled "Wine Tasting Notes" after its text seemed to "fit" with the glorious experience of tasting fine wines, including several such affairs at Richie and Cheryl Metrick's home in Lloyd Neck, New York—as illustrated by the featured menu that is part of the poem-sculpture. The poem is written against the white spaces within the illustration for Jeffrey E. Garten's article "Free Trade Has to Become Managed" in the July 18, 2001 *New York Times*. Initially, I thought the words to fit the poem due to the notion of an "expanding idea" (the poem's first line). Then I came to realize, too, that the Rohrschach-like shapes evoke wine spills.

    The sculpture came to include the *New York Times* article, "Live by the Pen, Die by the Sword," by John Noble Wilford on July 17, 2001. The article describes how, during the Maya civilization, scribes played a central role in magnifying their king's reputation—thought it apt as the notion of making "wine tasting notes" can magnify (both negatively and positively) the experience of wine tasting beyond the actual event. And because "fine wines" are a rarefied hobby. In any event, reading the entirety of the article against both poem and the experience of wine-tasting seemed to relate—an "integral" experience. Moreover, the orange-red cast of the illustration fits my memory of various wine-related experiences, e.g. the sunset over wine country(ies) or the faded red labels against old bottles or some shades of very old wine. After I utilized a cardboard box as the sculpture's "sleeve" I came to add the rattan pineapple coasters as their color and texture worked well against the cardboard and the newspaper illustration. Later, I thought to include various wine-related ephemera (a Bordeaux postcard from Rena Rosenwasser, an Ehlers Grove Winery, CA postcard, and a placement card from one of the Metricks' wine-imbibing dinners), partly to enliven the texture, references, and colors.

—Eileen R. Tabios

About the Poet

Eileen R. Tabios has released over 70 collections of poetry, fiction, essays, and experimental biographies from publishers around the world. Recent releases include the art monograph *Drawing The Six Directions*; a poetry collection *Because I Love You, I Become War*; an autobiography, *The Inventor;* and a flash fiction collection collaboration with harry k stammer, *Getting To One.* Other recent books include a first novel *DoveLion: A Fairy Tale for Our Times* which was subsequently translated by Danton Remoto into Filipino as *KalapatingLeon*; two French books, *PRISES* (*Double Take)* (trans. Fanny Garin) and *La Vie erotique de l'art* (trans. Samuel Rochery); and a book-length essay *Kapwa's Novels*. Her award-winning body of work includes invention of the hay(na)ku, a 21st century diasporic poetic form; the MDR Poetry Generator that can create poems totaling theoretical infinity; the "Flooid" poetry form that's rooted in a good deed; the monobon poetry form based on the monostich; and a first poetry book, *Beyond Life Sentences*, which received the Philippines' National Book Award for Poetry. Translated into 13 languages, she also has edited, co-edited or conceptualized 15 anthologies of poetry, fiction and essays. Her writing and editing works have received recognition through awards, grants and residencies.

More information is at http://eileenrtabios.com

Sandy Press

Sandy Press, a literary/arts publisher of innovative work, is co-edited by Mark Young and harry k stammer.

Current titles:

Mark Young
Ley Lines II
Threescore and Ten
Otoliths – May 2006 to August 2023
with the slow-paced turtle replaced by a fast fish
The Sasquatch Walks Among Us
sorties
XXXX Centones from the Cantos of EZRA POUND
Your order is now equipped for shipping
Songs to Come for the Salamander

harry k stammer
-48
walls 't'

Eileen R. Tabios
Getting To One – Flash Fictions by Eileen R. Tabios and Art by harry k stammer
Drawing The Six Directions

Sandy Press - Editors

Mark Young was born in New Zealand, & currently lives in a small town in North Queensland in Australia, but his books have been published across the world, from Scandinavia to the U.S.A. He has been publishing poetry for over sixty years, & is the author of around sixty books, primarily text poetry but also including speculative fiction, vispo, creative non-fiction, & art history. His work has been widely anthologized, & his essays & poetry translated into a number of languages.

harry k stammer is a writer and musician who lives and works in Santa Barbara, CA USA. He has published ten books of poetry and writes music for spoken poetry pieces. https://harrykstammer.bandcamp.com

www.ingramcontent.com/pod-product-compliance
Lightning Source LLC
Chambersburg PA
CBHW040223220526
45473CB00001B/97